I0540498

Change Your Mindset –
Think Like The Rich

Amit Eshet

Copyright © Amit Eshet

All rights reserved. No part of this book may be used or reproduced in any matter whatsoever without the written and signed permission.

Second Edition: 2017

ISBN: 978-965-92633-9-4

Publisher: Simple Story

www.simplestory.us

simplestory
Digital Publishing

TABLE OF CONTENTS

INTRODUCTION

Many customers ask me, "is it possible for me to get rich?" I tell them, "YES, you can!" But what I tell them next usually comes as a surprise for them —the road to richness begins in your *mind*.

If you have the wrong mindset, I can tell you right now that you'll never reach your goals. If your goal is to sit on your sofa watching TV and have someone knock on your door and give you a million dollars, you have the wrong mindset.

On the other hand, if you have a positive outlook and feel like you deserve to be rich, then you're already headed in the right direction! Those who are active and ambitious already have the tools that they need to succeed.

Many people afraid of money, but there is no need to stress. This book will give you 36 thoughtful phrases that show the difference in thinking between the average person, and the rich.

In the following pages you will find at least one point that will help YOU change your mindset and start thinking like the rich!

Every day in a month read one phrase and implement it in your life.

Good Luck!

POINT 1:

DON'T LET THE OPINIONS OF AVERAGE PEOPLE SWAY YOU.

Dream - and they think you are crazy

Succeed - and they think you are lucky

Acquire wealth - and they say you are greedy

Pay no attention, they simply don't understand.

Most people are scared of change, afraid of the unknown and even afraid to succeed.

Full of good intentions they want to protect you and wish you only the best, but they may scare you and make you believe they are right.

With their love they are stopping you.

The rich believe in their own way and do not let anyone distract them from their orbit. They have confidence in their way, they are prepared to be wrong from time to time but they are convinced they will reach their destination.

They do not let anyone get to them, scare them and divert them from the path they believe in.

POINT 2:

WHAT IS YOUR POINT OF VIEW ON MONEY?

Most people think that money is the root of all evil;

That it overcomplicates life and leads to stress, fighting, and the loss of loved ones. But, this is the mindset that you need to change if you want to start thinking like the rich.

The rich believe that poverty is the root of all evil;

That without money you cannot take care of your family or make the most out of your life with friends. Rich people see money as a way to enjoy more of life with the ones around you, not as a stressor that makes life less enjoyable.

POINT 3:

DO YOU USE ACTIONS, OR WORDS?

For most of us, complaining is a form a therapy;

An everyday part of life that may be cathartic, but accomplishes absolutely nothing.

For rich people, DOING is the answer to everything.

They understand that nothing is ever achieved merely by complaining about it. If they want something, they will do whatever they need to do in order to get it done. Action, not words, is what helps the rich rake in their wealth.

POINT 4:

Every morning in Africa a gazelle wakes up.
She knows she must run faster than the fastest lion,
Otherwise she will end her life.
Every morning in Africa a lion wakes up.
He knows he must run faster than the slowest gazelle,
Otherwise he'll starve to death.

NO MATTER IF YOU ARE A LION OR A GAZELLE, WHEN THE SUN COMES UP, YOU BETTER START RUNNING

Most people have a belief: What happened in the past will happen again in the future.

This limiting belief makes them not want to do anything else, and think that things are just going to be fine.

They blame the government, the employer and the neighbors and are not willing to take responsibility.

The rich understand that everything depends on them, no matter if they are a lion or gazelle – they are running.

They want to affect their future wealth by themselves.

POINT 5:

"SUCCESS IS THE ABILITY TO MOVE FROM ONE FAILURE TO ANOTHER WITHOUT LOSING ENTHUSIASM"

Winston Churchill

Most people do not believe. They just don't have faith. They do not believe it will get better, they do not believe they can be happy and they do not believe they can get rich. At times they are willing to try something new, but if they fail they immediately get the feeling of "I told you I can't do it, I told you the whole world is against us."

The rich understand that you can't succeed without failing along the way. They dared, tried and failed.

But if you learn from your failures and continue to move forward with the enthusiasm of a child taking his first steps, you can reach much wealth and happiness.

POINT 6:

"IT'S NOT A SHAME TO BE BORN POOR, BUT IT IS SHAME TO DIE POOR"

BILL GATES

Most people find it difficult to get out of the environment in which they were raised and educated. If you grow up in a poor environment they feel their destiny to be poor and to suffer, for whole life.

Wealthy people, by nature, do not give up. They understand that their parent's sufferings do not mean they have to suffer as well.

They strive to move forward and don't let any obstacles stop them from reaching the wealth and prosperity they desire.

They honestly believe they deserve more and that they are good enough. Those who believe in it succeed in achieving it!

POINT 7:

WHAT IS YOUR STANCE ON FORMAL EDUCATION?

Most of us go through life being taught that the road to riches is paved with formal education;

That without college and educational training, we will never amount to anything.

We learn without exact goal, and try a little bit from everything.

The rich, however, believe in acquiring specific knowledge.

They understand that a lot of broad general knowledge will not do much, but learning a LOT about a particular subject will make them an expert. Being able to be an expert leads to the ability to earn greater amounts of money.

POINT 8:

IF WEALTH WAS THE DIRECT RESULT OF HARD WORK, EVERY WOMAN IN AFRICA WOULD BE A MILLIONAIRE.

Most people feel that if they only work harder, spend more hours at work and continue working from home at night, their wealth and financial situation will improve.

Rich people know that you don't need to work hard in order to get rich. You need to understand what it takes and find ways to get rich without having to work hard all day, all year round.

Do you want proof?

Think about the African women's wealth…

POINT 9:

WOULD YOU RATHER BE ENTERTAINED, OR EDUCATED?

Most people would rather be entertained than educated.

After work time sitting front of TV and waiting for the next comedy show.

Rich people would rather be educated than entertained.

They realize that in order to reach their greatest earning ability, they need to absorb as much information as possible—entertainment is secondary, as it adds little to their lives in terms of value.

POINT 10:

WHAT IS YOUR RELATIONSHIP WITH MONEY?

For most of us, dealing with money is an emotional process.

We agonize over how much we have, we worry, we stress, and most of the time unnecessarily. Money is seen as a catalyst for troubles, or a catalyst for happiness.

Rich people think about money logically.

It is used to purchase needed items; it is an investment tool, not an emotional burden.

Money served their dreams and ideas for making more money.

Money is a play toy for the rich.

POINT 11:

ANYONE WHO WANTS TO MAKE A LIVING HAS TO WORK.

THOSE WHO WANT TO GET RICH HAVE TO FIND ANOTHER WAY.

Most people think that the only way to make money is to go to work.

Get up early in the morning, work all day and come home in the evening tired and exhausted.

Most people live from weekend to weekend and wait for the holiday season to rest. Work will get you a respectable livelihood but will not get you wealth.

The rich understand that working hard brings a livelihood but not wealth. To get rich you need to find sources of passive income such as rent for example.

Another way to get rich is through investment, after you understood and learned the investment market. You can of course start a company and hire employees to work for you, so you'll have time to spend the money and get rich.

The rich understand that you can't earn and make big money by working 9-5, so let's join them.

POINT 12: TIME

"EVERYDAY IS A BANK ACCOUNT AND TIME IS OUR CURRENCY. NO ONE IS RICH, NO ONE IS POOR, WE'VE GOT 24 HOURS EACH."

CHRISTOPHER RICE

Because of stress we sometimes forget that the gift we were all given is the same: 24 hours a day.

Have you ever thought how much is it 1440 minutes a day, every day?

How much can you get done in 1,440 minutes?

Rich people treat every day, every minute, as if it's their last and try to get as much as possible out of it.

Too many people say, why go now? Why run and try? I don't have a chance, maybe tomorrow will be better, and more excuses like these.

What type of person are you?

POINT 13:

BEFORE YOU SPEAK, LISTEN

BEFORE YOU WRITE, THINK

BEFORE YOU SPEND, EARN

BEFORE YOU INVEST, INVESTIGATE

BEFORE YOU BLAME, TRY

BEFORE YOU RETIRE, SAVE.

Respect others, get used to looking one step ahead and do not be one who "lives the moment, because you only live once".

This is true in all areas of life, but forward vision has even greater significance in the financial world.

Thinking ahead and long-term planning of your income and expenses, will lead to wealth and serenity.

Your financial future cannot be ignored, it will be here much faster than you think.

Your standard of living when you retire depends only on you!!

POINT 14:

"TOO MANY PEOPLE SPEND MONEY THEY HAVEN'T EARNED, TO BUY THINGS THEY DON'T WANT, TO IMPRESS PEOPLE THAT THEY DON'T LIKE."

WILL ROGERS

Question: How many times have you done something you really didn't like and didn't want to do, but still did it because you didn't want to appear different??

How many times did you buy a fashionable item you didn't really like just because it is the fashion at the moment?

Most people want to be sociable and be okay with everyone. Being an exception is not an option in their eyes so often they do things they do not believe in, just to obtain the environment's seal of approval.

Riche people lead with their opinions. They go after their truth and don't care what other people think about them.

They want to do only what they want and they believe it will advance them to further success.

Think like the rich means going forward with your truth to the end.

POINT 15:

MANY PEOPLE LOOK AT WEALTH AND ASSETS AS SOMETHING EVIL. SOMETHING THEY WISH WASN'T USED AS A MEASUREMENT IN OUR WORLD.

Wealth and assets bring with them many frustrations and result in feelings on anger and disappointment.

The rich understand that wealth and assets are part of life, if not the best part. They are happy to have more of it.

We should look at wealth and money as a form of life energy, a form of energy we can't survive without.

Those who understand that fortune and money are a form of energy and invites it into their lives – life smiles back at them and everything looks and feels more relaxed and pleasant.

POINT 16:

WHAT DO YOU THINK IS REQUIRED IN ORDER TO MAKE MONEY?

Most of us believe that in order to make money, you need to already have large sums of money.

Money to pay for the best team of workers, to pay for the highest quality materials, to get people to take notice of you at all. In this mindset you believe that without money, no one will look your way in the business realm.

Rich people are able to preserve their money by using other people's money. How do they do this? By getting others to invest money in their cause. Using strategic communication, the rich are able to use the money of others first, THEN have their own funds to fall back on—not the other way around!

POINT 17:

"BEING RICH IS NOT ABOUT HOW MUCH MONEY YOU HAVE OR HOW MANY HOMES YOU OWN; IT'S THE FREEDOM TO BUY ANY BOOK YOU WANT WITHOUT LOOKING AT THE PRICE AND WONDERING IF YOU CAN AFFORD IT."

JOHN WATERS

Most people think being rich means you have a lot of houses, a lot of money in the bank and you travel in luxury cars.

A real rich person is the one who feels he has what it takes without thinking twice whether he can afford it or not.

If you believe wealth starts with your heart, you'll get material wealth much faster than you though possible.

POINT 18:

WHAT BELIEFS DO YOU INSTILL IN YOUR CHILDREN?

Most people teach their children how to grow up and survive as adults in the "real world"—how to get through school successfully, get jobs, save money, and be responsible.

Rich people teach their kids to get rich.

For them, it's not so much about how to grow emotionally— it's how to grow financially. The belief of the rich is that as long as a person has money, they will be able to take care of themselves.

POINT 19:

HOW DO YOU VIEW RICH PEOPLE?

Most people think that rich people are snobs who only wish to associate with other rich people.

Generally, we believe that rich people are looking down upon those who are less fortunate as pitiful, soft individuals.

However, rich people just want to surround themselves with like-minded people.

It's simple—most people want to be around people who they are similar too. "Birds of a feather flock together" goes the saying, and it's true for the rich as well. The rich will have more in common with other rich people than they will with the poor, or the middle-class.

POINT 20:

THE PERSON WHO DOESN'T KNOW WHERE HIS NEXT DOLLAR IS COMING FROM USUALLY DOESN'T KNOW WHERE HIS LAST DOLLAR WENT TO.

No matter what befalls us, we human beings are a gullible and optimistic animal. The same goes for our relationship with money; those who don't have much feel that no matter what they'll do, they will never have enough. So why bother?

"Things will be okay, somehow we'll manage...." Usually it doesn't work that way and those who don't think about tomorrow end up heavy in debt, loans and have to lower their standard of living.

The rich know they must plan. They have to know what the cash flow is, how much money they have, how much they can take, how much they will invest and how much they will save.

By planning and thinking about income and expenses you can increase your fortune and become rich.

POINT 21:

DO YOU FEEL THAT YOU CAN HAVE EITHER FAMILY OR MONEY?

Most people believe that they need to choose between their family, and being rich.

The general thought process is that one cannot have both, because it is too time-consuming to spend quality time with your family and spend the hours required working to make money.

Rich people on the other hand know that it is possible to have both.

Having a family who understands that working is a form of caring for them, who understands that you work so hard to earn large sums of money in order to give them a better, more lavish life is possible.

Time management is the key of success.

POINT 22:

WHAT IS YOUR VIEW OF THE FINANCIAL MARKET?

Most people believe that financial markets are driven by logic and strategy, and that the only way to succeed when it comes to stocks and investments is to have a trained financial ninja with inside information and carefully calculated predictions.

Rich people know that the market is driven primarily by emotion and greed. Without these feelings, the market would never budge. Greed leads to action in the financial market, action leads to results and the rich are results driven.

POINT 23:

"A PENNY SAVED IS A PENNY EARNED"

BENJAMIN FRANKLIN

Most people tend to underestimate small amounts.
When they are offered a small discount they say: "It is so small, what difference does it make?"

That is a big mistake and the wrong behavior.

The rich realize there is no such thing as small change.
Even saving of $10 per month, equals to $120 a year. After 10 years the saving will accumulate to $1,200.

Savings of $1,200 is a substantial amount for everyone.

The rich know that money accumulates and therefore their approach to savings is to accumulate small savings into large savings and wealth.

POINT 24:

"THE STARTING POINT OF ALL ACHIEVEMENT IS DESIRE. KEEP THIS CONSTANTLY IN MIND. WEAK DESIRE BRINGS WEAK RESULTS, JUST AS A SMALL FIRE MAKES A SMALL AMOUNT OF HEAT."

NAPOLEON HILL

Most people do not believe they can make a difference. They do not believe they can change themselves, their environment or their financial situation.

The rich understand that everything starts with the passion. If we believe in our way and our desires - we succeed.

Small bumpy roads will not divert us from where we are going.

Inner belief and a burning internal fire will bring about success.

POINT 25:

WHAT IS YOUR VIEW ON SAVINGS?

Most peoples' financial focus is on saving the money that they have;

Holding onto it and not spending it frivolously. While saving is important, the rich do not let it dominate their financial plans.

Instead, the rich focus their efforts on earning more, not worrying about saving every penny they can. With the focus on earning, the amount saved is insignificant in comparison to the amount of money constantly coming in.

POINT 26:

HOW DO YOU FEEL ABOUT YOUR JOB?

Most people make a living by going to a job they earns a respectable salary, but isn't a profession that they feel truly passionate about.

Rich people on the other hand are able to make so much money because they make a living doing what they love, and what they are good at. Passion is a major factor in earning large sums of money because it creates lasting power. When a person does what he or she loves, they can do it for many years without burning out like people in "everyday" jobs.

POINT 27:

DO YOU VIEW MONEY AS A STRESSOR?

For most people, money is a stressor.

It becomes the biggest burden in their lives; constantly worrying over whether or not there is enough money to cover all their expenses. Often times, along with financial worries comes the stress of making tough choices when it comes to luxuries that need to be given up.

On the other hand, the rich do not view money as a catalyst for stress. Instead, **they view money as opportunities** to experience life to the fullest. Money is seen as a window to the luxuries in life, not as a burden that gets rid of those luxuries.

POINT 28:

"IT IS NOT ENOUGH THAT WE DO OUR BEST; SOMETIMES WE MUST DO WHAT IS REQUIRED"

WINSTON CHURCHILL

The majority of people work very hard, bring up a family and occasionally go out to enjoy themselves.

Some of them travel abroad and experience new experiences and faraway worlds, some of them go on camping trips closer to home.

Between work, family and recreation they do not have time or energy to do anything.

That's not entirely true, they also watch television, go to the beach and meet up with friends to grumble.

They are so busy running from place to place that they have no free time.

Rich people understand that the most important quality is differentiating between the significant and the insignificant.

They will constantly ask themselves: Will what I am currently doing really help me with anything?

Does this action bring me closer to the goal?

They will never say: That's life, there's nothing we can do about it. They will not waste their time on meaningless activities which leave them with no time for the really important things.

They will be focused on the future and concentrate on things which will bring them riches and success.

The trick is to combine pleasure with clear goals.

POINT 29:

"LIFE IS ABOUT BALANCE. THE GOOD AND THE BAD. THE HIGHS AND THE LOWS. THE THING EVERYONE SHOULD REALIZE IS THAT THE KEY TO HAPPINESS IS BEING HAPPY BY YOURSELF AND FOR YOURSELF. HAPPINESS COMES FROM WITHIN. YOU HAVE THE POWER TO CHANGE YOUR OWN MINDSET SO THAT ALL THE NEGATIVE, HORRIBLE THOUGHTS THAT TRY TO INVADE YOUR PSYCHE ARE REPLACED WITH HAPPY, POSITIVE, WONDERFUL THOUGHTS."

ELLEN DEGENERES

Our success, wealth and happiness - It all starts within us. We choose whether to be insulted by the things we were told.

We choose to get up with a smile in the morning or get up tired and disgruntled.

We choose whether to smile to friends at work and to the cashier at the supermarket.

A rich person knows that everything depends on him, and if he feels happy and projects a sense of pleasure and happiness - his wealth is guaranteed.

We are responsible for ourselves!!!

POINT 30:

"MONEY IS ONLY A TOOL. IT WILL TAKE YOU WHEREVER YOU WISH, BUT IT WILL NOT REPLACE YOU AS THE DRIVER".

AYN RAND

Most people believe that if they win the lottery or receive a large inheritance, their lives will change and everything will work out.

They think money buys everything and runs everything, and solves all problems.

The rich realize that money can indeed buy a lot of things, but they need to manage their fortune and know where to invest.

Diversification of investments at an appropriate risk level is what will keep your fortune growing. As long as you navigate correctly and know where your money is, the future will look good.

POINT 31:

NEVER GAMBLE WITH YOUR MONEY. GAMBLING DOES NOT LEAD TO WEALTH.

Many people who have less money than they would like search for a quick solution: gambling.

This could be gambling on the lottery, or in casinos.

They do so in the hope that "Any minute my luck will change and I'll become rich."

They usually lose large amounts of money which, as you recall, they did not have in the first place.

Rich people know that there are no shortcuts.

You need to map out a path to wealth and follow it. The rich person knows that he must manage his money and not rely on the goddess of fortune.

The rich person invests his money, and only takes loans after ensuring he will be able to repay them; he never wagers with his money simply out of a desire to gamble and in the hope of becoming rich quickly and easily.

POINT 32:

"MONEY IS NOT EVERYTHING AS LONG AS YOU HAVE ENOUGH".

MALCOM FORBES

We are all familiar with the 'eat and drink as tomorrow you will die' lifestyle.

You only live once, so why save and why worry?

This is all well and good as long as we have enough money to support ourselves and our family.

Most people do not imagine that anything could go wrong, so they allow themselves to buy whatever they want, to take out large loans without thinking how they will repay them and to act in a financially extravagant manner.

Rich people understand that nothing is eternal, and that everything could change suddenly.

Therefore, they always have money put aside for a rainy day.

This is what helps them to continue to advance and progress even during difficult financial periods.

POINT 33:

"IF I AM NOT FOR MYSELF, WHO IS FOR ME..."

ETHICS OF THE FATHERS 1:14

Too many people rely on luck.

They think that they will be taken care of – but forget to ask themselves who exactly will do so.

They think that everything will always be okay, and rely on their improvisational abilities.

They think that they "deserve" everything because they pay taxes, served in the army and are good citizens.

Rich people understand that no one will take care of them if they do not take care of themselves.

Rich people understand that they need to make plans and look to the future, and they do not wait for miracles and fortune to appear on their doorstep.

A rich person knows what is happening with his money, he sets himself aspirations and goals and plans the means to achieve them.

POINT 34:

ONE WHO INCREASES POSSESSIONS INCREASES WORRY

ETHICS OF THE FATHERS

Many people mistakenly understand this sentence as saying: It is better to be poor, without many possessions, as then you will be worry-free.

Really?

Is someone who has no money, nothing to eat and nowhere to live worry-free?

Is bravery saying no to yourself and your children because you don't have enough money?

Rich people know that having no money and possessions is a much greater problem than having a fortune and managing it.

The rich person can employ professional management services, or manage his assets himself, and most importantly: He is not worried where next month's salary will come from.

POINT 35:

"HE WHO RELIES ON GUARANTEED PROFITS, HIS WEALTH WILL NOT FLOURISH

AND HE WHO INVESTS HIS ENERGY IN ADVENTURES, POVERTY IS LIKELY TO AWAIT HIM AROUND THE CORNER.

A PERSON SHOULD ENCLOSE THE ADVENTURE IN A GUARANTEED FENCE WHICH WILL GUARD HIM FROM LOSSES."

SIR FRANCIS BACON

Most people hate to lose. We despise losing more than we love winning.

A few people "go all out". They don't care about tomorrow, they live the here and now.

Anyone who wants to earn money and become rich needs to find the balance between the two approaches.

Being anxious and scared of losing money – will never lead to riches.

In the financial world, chances and risks go hand in hand: a low risk = a small chance of large profits.

One who wants to throw everything he has into something and then leave may find himself penniless and impoverished, for as we have said: a large chance = a high risk.

Genuinely rich people invest a large proportion of their wealth in secure channels, and use a small proportion of their money to seek out adventures which will increase their capital and expand their wealth.

POINT 36:

MINDS ARE LIKE FLOWERS, THEY ONLY OPEN WHEN THE TIME IS RIGHT

In this book, I tried to help you better understand how you can influence your future.

If you believe that you deserve more, you deserve only the good and to be wealthy - you will succeed.

My experience as financial planner shows me this: It is all up to you!!!

I wish you all the best and much success toward wealth and happiness.

Amit Eshet

www.ingramcontent.com/pod-product-compliance
Lightning Source LLC
Chambersburg PA
CBHW071543120626
46550CB00006B/2564